KEITH SYLER
Illustrated by
JULIE SNEEDEN

WHEN A LOBSTER WHISTLES!

Never-Ending Love Around the World

For mom.

Everyone says it differently,
but they mean the same thing...

Never-ending love
can make your heart sing!

I'm Madi. I live in the United States.
Dad tells me he will love me
always and forever.
That's the opposite of never!

Daddy tells me,
"I will only
stop loving you...
...when pigs fly!"

That's cuckoo!
In French, that's *completement fou!*
I know pigs can't fly!
I'm Jean-Christophe. I live in France.
When Mom sees me,
she says her heart flutters.

She tells me,
"I will only stop loving you...
quand les poules auront les dents!"
In French that means...

*...when chickens
have teeth!*

But she says, even if I did,
she would only stop loving me...
...balik ağaca çikinca !
In Turkish, that means...

...when fish
climb trees!

Fish don't climb trees. That's *loco!*
I'm Raul, and I live in the Dominican Republic.
Sometimes I go fishing with my uncle.
We sit in a boat on days that I wish
would never end. But they always do.

When I complain,
he says one thing will never end...
"I will only stop loving you when
...*la marrana ponga huevos!*"
In Spanish that means...

Pigs can't lay eggs!
I'm Arnoldo and I'm from Bolivia.
I speak Spanish, too, but I checked with my mom
and I know for a fact that pigs never lay eggs.

Mom also told me something else
that will never happen.
She said, "Arnie, I will only stop loving you...
...*cuando a las ranas les salgan pelos!*"
In Spanish, that means...

*...when frogs
grow hair!*

I've never seen a hairy frog! That's a bit *gek*.
I'm Anneke. I live in the Netherlands.
In Dutch, *"gek"* is how we say crazy.
Hairy frogs? What a *gek* thing!
My mom would never say that.
But she does often say
she would only stop loving me...
"...als de koeien op het ijs dansen!"
In Dutch, that means...

I'm Somchai. And I'm Apinya.
We're twins, and we live in Thailand.
We've never seen cows dance on ice...
but we don't get much ice in Thailand,
so you never know.

Dad says he's crazy about us,
even when we are double trouble.
In fact, he says he will
only stop loving us...
"Bāy waṇ h̄nụ̀ng nı kārk lạb
chāti mā keid k̄hxng khuṇ"
In Thai, that means...

...one afternoon in
your next reincarnation!
(...which means never!)

My name is Tatyana. I'm from Russia.
I don't know much about reincarnation
except that it is a big word.
I do know one thing, though.

Mom says she will only stop loving me...
"Kogda omar svistit na vershine gory!"
In Russian, that means...

...when a lobster
whistles
on top of
a mountain!

Do lobsters even have lips?
I'm Erik, and I live with my auntie in Denmark.
She whistles funny songs while she cleans the house.

When I help her, she says,
"Erik, I will only stop loving you...
når der er to torsdage i en uge!"
In Danish, that means...

Who ever heard of two Thursdays in a week?
I'm Hans, and I live in Germany.
My dad says if he could have
two of the same days, he'd choose Saturday.
That's his day off!

Dad tells me he likes days off
because he can spend time with Mom and me.

I heard Dad say something sweet
to Mom just last night.
Dad said he would only stop loving her...
"wenn es im sommer schneit!"
In German, that means...

*...when it
snows
in summer!*

It doesn't snow in summer!
I'm Goutham. I live in India.
In my hometown, it's only hot.
We've never even seen snow!
Mom tells me I may see snow
somewhere else, someday.

But wherever I might go,
one thing will never change...

She says, "I will only stop loving you when...
kakka marannu parakkuka!"
In Malayalam, that means...

...when the crow flies upside down!

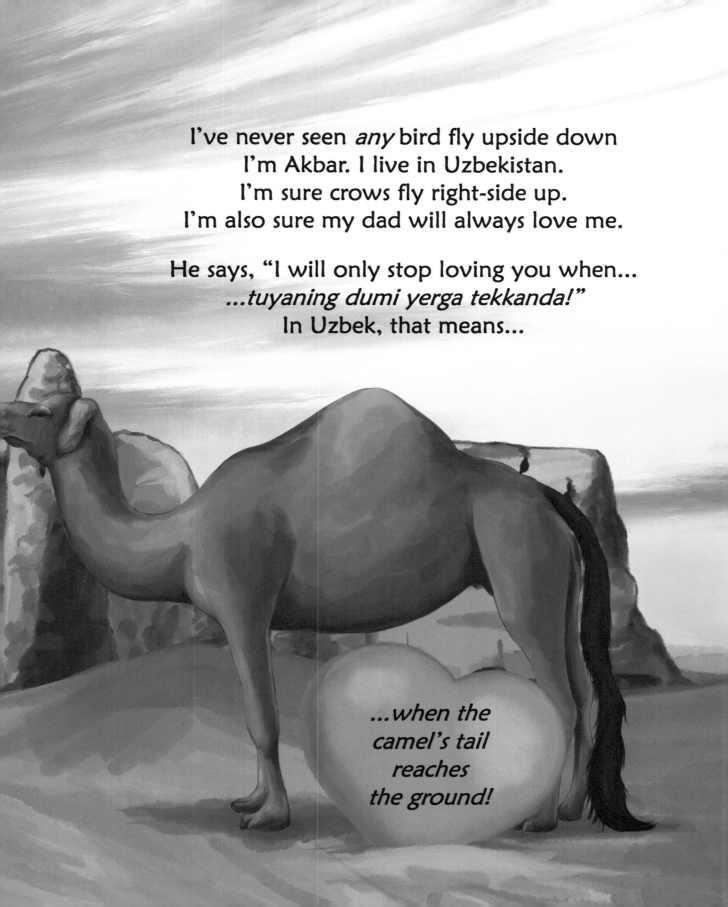

I've never seen *any* bird fly upside down
I'm Akbar. I live in Uzbekistan.
I'm sure crows fly right-side up.
I'm also sure my dad will always love me.

He says, "I will only stop loving you when...
...*tuyaning dumi yerga tekkanda!*"
In Uzbek, that means...

...when the camel's tail reaches the ground!

Some things will simply *never* happen.

Pigs won't fly...
...and crows won't fly upside-down.
There are a million songs
that a lobster will never whistle.

But there's one thing for sure...
Wherever you go,
and however you may hear it said...

The way you are loved
by those who love you most
is something you can
carry in your heart
always and forever.

Love never ends!

PRONOUNCE THE WORDS!

Use these phonetic pronunciations
or an online tool and say it like a local.

French: **complètement fou**

KUM-pleht-maw foo

quand les poules auront les dents

kahn lay puul oor-AHN lay dawn

Turkish: **balik ağaca çikinca**

BAH-leek ah-CHAH chee-KIHN-jah

Spanish: **loco**

LOH-koh

la marrana ponga huevos

La ma-RAN-a PONG-a WHEH-vohs

cuando a las ranas les salgan pelos

KWAHN-do ah las RAN-as lay sahl-gahn PAY-lohs

Dutch: **gek**

HEHK

als de koeien op het ijs dansen

AHLS deh KOO-ee-yehn ohp eht EHS dahn-she

Thai: ่บ่ายวันหนึ่งในการกลับชาติมาเกิดของคุณ

(B̀āy wạn h̄nừng nı kārk lạb chāti mā keid k̄hxng khuṇ)

BEYE wun ning nay kahn klahp
TAH mah keh kran-taw eye kohn-koon

Russian: когда омар свистит на вершине горы

(Kogda omar svistit na vershine gory)

KAHG-dah oh-mar svees-TEET neh verr-SHEEN-eh gar-eh

Danish: når der er to torsdage i en uge

nah DAR toh toh-STAY ehn oo

German: wenn es im sommer schneit

VEHN ehs ehm ZUH-mah SHNEYET

Malayalam: കാക്ക മാറന്നു പറക്കുക

(Kakka marannu parakkuka)

KAH-ka ma-REH-noo par-AH-koh-ka

Uzbek: tuyaning dumi yerga tekkanda

TOO-yah-ni doo-meh yair-gah the-kan-daa

AFTERWORD

Different languages use different alphabets, with different accents, and even different letters for sounds that aren't used in other languages. The English language uses the Roman Alphabet. Russian uses Cyrillic. Malayalam uses a Brahmic script; Thai uses an abugida writing script.

Sometimes, in every language, we use expressions called idioms. Idioms are a collection of words that mean something different together than the literal words on their own. You aren't really referring to pigs actually flying when you use the expression, you mean "never."

Idioms can be funny and hard to understand in any language. "When pigs fly" and "When a lobster whistles on top of a mountain" are also something called an adynaton. That's a figure of speech of such exaggeration taken to extreme lengths so as to mean a complete impossibility.

Scholars think the idea of flying pigs arose in Germany or Scotland. Cincinnati, Ohio, where many German immigrants settled, became known as "Porkopolis" by the 1830s due to its meat-packing industry. That industry has declined, but Cincinnati hosts the "Flying Pig Marathon" now, every year. Some runners run in pig suits to show that in their city, they believe just about anything is possible. The author, though now a Raven, thinks they might be right. Who dey!

ABOUT THE CHARACTERS

Some of the characters in this book are named after real people the author met during his travels.

Madi is a teacher with Baltimore County Schools, in Maryland, USA.

Jean-Christophe, "JC," works in finance and international management.

Emin works in tourism and agriculture.

Raul is a professional dancer and acrobat.

Arnoldo is the middle name of Carlos, an artist and instructor of fine arts and ceramics.

Anneke works in commercial insurance.

Tatyana is a businesswoman and foster youth advocate.

Goutham is a urologic oncologist.

ABOUT THE AUTHOR

Inspired by his friends from around the world, their languages and cultures, **KEITH SYLER** revels in our human diversity and commonality. Having lived in West Africa, Europe, Canada, and having circled the globe, he has seen a lot of families and people who love one another with never-ending love. He's also experienced it.

Keith grew up in Fredericktown, Ohio, and later studied law, business, and journalism. He immersed himself in French in Québec, and Spanish in both the Dominican Republic and Colombia. As a lawyer in Cincinnati, he worked for twelve years as a federal law clerk to the late Hon. S. Arthur Spiegel; as a whistleblower lawyer; and as a tenant advocate.

Keith currently lives in Baltimore, Maryland, where he volunteers in welcoming new Americans, and he works with other Presbyterians to advocate for Cubans. He has assisted teachers in the public schools, and he sometimes lifeguards with the real-life Madi from the opening of this book.

ABOUT THE ILLUSTRATOR

Constantly inspired by the words and tales of imaginative authors, **JULIE SNEEDEN** uses color, light and creativity to bring her artwork into these magical worlds. To make the character of her images come to life, she draws upon a palette of tools including watercolor, pencil, charcoal, digital illustration, photography, and oil paints.

Julie studied Fine Arts in KwaZulu Natal, South Africa, but now lives with her family in the UK. Reading stories to her children has inspired her over the years to pursue the art of illustration. She has illustrated numerous stories to amazing authors all over the world.

ISBN: 978-1-64649-333-3 (paperback)

ISBN: 978-1-64649-335-7 (hardcover)

Printed in the USA
CPSIA information can be obtained
at www.ICGtesting.com
LVHW071047310823
756760LV00012B/167